INTERTWINING
CHOICES

A Curriculum of Social Acquisition and Empowerment

Cleresse Sprague

PAGE PUBLISHING, INC.
New York, NY

First originally published by Page Publishing, Inc. 2017

ISBN 978-1-63568-957-0 (Paperback)
ISBN 978-1-63568-958-7 (Digital)

Printed in the United States of America

FOREWORD

In today's society, our youth have an array of social issues they are trying to cope with and to comprehend. A long-time friend may suddenly turn against them, or the devastation they feel day after day in a perceived hostile environment can lead to suicide. Our youth may be confused, searching for answers, and in need of guidance.

Parents, families, school staff, the juvenile justice system, organized youth groups, and the medical profession are all educators who impact the social development of our youth. Situations can arise suddenly that leave these educators confused and in search of information that will help them guide our youth in a positive and comprehensible manner.

Intertwining Choices is a curriculum developed to enhance social acquisition and empowerment for our youth as they traverse into the realm of adulthood. The Intertwining Choices curriculum is comprised of social stories complete with study guides. The curriculum is designed to help our youth reflect on social issues while helping educators guide them through the process of comprehending the dilemmas associated with these social situations.

CONTENTS

FRIENDS:
BEYOND TIME AND
THROUGHOUT ETERNITY

PROLOGUE

This is a story of friendship. It is a story that encompasses love and misunderstanding, happiness, and sadness. This story is intended to foster self-reflection and an awareness of the value of friendship.

We had been friends since the first day of kindergarten. I remember sitting on the log, my heart breaking as Dad drove away after leaving me in "the very good hands" of Mrs. Trundle.

Angela was the first to approach me. She looked at me once and then again. One tear slipped from her eye and rolled down her check as she sat next to me on the log. Angela reached out and put a small cold hand on top of mine. We sat together for what seemed an eternity.

The school bell rang as we continued to sit. Samantha approached us and reached out her hands. Angela and I each took a warm little hand and walked with Samantha into the school. That simple gesture was to launch the three of us into a friendship that would lead us through a cavern of uncertainty and return us to the light of the sun.

Throughout kindergarten we were inseparable. As long as we were together nothing could "rattle" our world. We worked, played, ate and sang songs as one. When one of us was sick, we were all sick. Life couldn't have been any better.

Each year through fourth grade saw our friendship grow deeper. It was unimaginable to believe that anything on earth could have rocked this friendship. Even in the eyes of our families, we were a unit of one.

We began fifth grade year feeling ablaze with excitement. We were in a new school. We anticipated meeting new classmates and making new friends, yet knowing that our friendship was unshakable. Little did we know at the time that this friendship would be tested beyond the boundaries of our experiences.

It started quite simply. A little teasing, directed mostly at Angela. She was easy to tease with her sweet way of blushing and never seemingly to be upset.

Sometimes there was a tear in Angela's eye, but that was easy to explain. She was just too sensitive.

As the school year progressed Samantha and I got more and more caught up in letting our new friends lead the way and dictate our actions. Angela was still our best friend, but she didn't seem to be making the right choices. When Angela would wear an outfit like ours or chose the same colors, she was a copycat. If Angela would be honest with a teacher about an event that happened, she was a tattletale. When Angela wouldn't sneak out with us and go to the movies, she was a baby.

Samantha and I were on and off again with our new friends. When it was an "off" day, Angela made great choices and she could do no wrong. When it was an "on" day, Angela's choices were bad and we needed to teach her a lesson by avoiding her.

Angela never understood the new rules. Friendship to Angela meant complete loyalty and total support. If Samantha or I were hurt, Angela was there to pick us up. When we had a "bad hair day" she reminded us of the one or two hairs that looked perfect. If we were grounded and couldn't go see the newest movie, Angela would wait patiently until we were able to go with her.

Angela was the truest of all friends. She would have given her life for us. Samantha and I didn't know the depth of Angela's friendship until it was too late.

The day started as an "on" day. Angela showed up at school wearing two pony tails in her hair. Samantha and I along with our new friends were all wearing two pony tails in our hair. Angela of course was a copycat because she really only liked one pony tail in her hair. As the day progressed Angela made those bad choices. When the teacher asked Angela who was making the rude noises in class, she named one of our new friends who had to then serve some detention time during recess.

Angela of course was a tattletale, she could have lied to the teacher. Angela refused to write the teacher's name together with a swear word on the bathroom wall. Of course Angela was a baby and it was time to teach her that lesson again by avoiding her.

We were really only teaching Angela a lesson. She needed to know what true friendship really meant. When the day ended Angela asked to walk home from school with us. We were all sure she hadn't learned her lesson yet so we continued avoiding her. Angela turned away from us, but not before I saw the one single tear roll down her cheek and drop onto her shirt collar.

No one knows where the car came from, but in one single instant life changed forever.

How we got there I don't know, but Samantha and I were in the hospital emergency room with Angela. Due to the gravity of the situation we were allowed in to see her. As Samantha and I each sat on one side of her, Angela opened her eyes. A tear rolled down her cheek and onto the pillow. She put one small cold hand on top of each of our hands. "Friends beyond time and throughout eternity." Those were the last words Angela would ever speak. As her eyes closed, so did her life on earth.

I came to understand friendship because of the loss of my dearest friend. Angela wasn't being a copycat when she dressed like the rest of us or wore her hair the same. She was simply showing that she valued us as being very special and she was proud to identify with us. Angela wasn't being a tattletale when she told the truth about what happened. She was being honest just as she had been shown through family values. Angela wasn't being a baby when she wouldn't do something that she knew was wrong. She was demonstrating the respect she had always been taught.

Angela is in my heart and in my very soul. Having Angela as a friend and understanding the value of a true friendship is the greatest gift I have ever received.

STUDY GUIDE

GLOSSARY OF TERMS

ablaze—glowing

anticipated—looked forward to an event with happiness

beloved—greatly loved; dear to the heart

cavern of uncertainty—not knowing what the outcome of a situation will be

encompassed—to include completely

eternity—something that lasts forever

foster—to promote the growth of something

gesture—a movement that expresses an idea

gravity—very serious

inseparable—not wanting to be apart

patiently—able and willing to wait for something to happen

self—reflection—using past events to help in understanding a current situation

sensitive—easily hurt or offended

unimaginable—unable to believe that something could happen

PRE/POST DISCUSSION QUESTIONS

The questions are intended to be used before the story to generate a discussion about friendship and after the story to measure any impact the story may have had on the students' views of friendship.

1. What does friendship mean to you?
2. What kind of person do you want your friend to be?
3. What kind of a person do you think your friend wants you to be?
4. What kind of a friend are you?
5. Do you have to choose sides between two friends?

Extended Activities:

*   Rewrite the ending to this story starting when the girls were in fifth grade.
*   Write a play for this story using a different ending.
*   Have a special "friend party" in the class and invite a friend to attend with you.
*   Establish pen pals in a neighboring school and invite them to visit your class.

NOTES

THE GIFT WITHIN

PROLOGUE

Lessons. We all learn them. Some lessons are small ones and we simply add them to our repertoire of lessons learned. We call on those lessons from time to time. Some lessons are bigger ones that help us in our daily functioning as human beings. Occasionally in a lifetime we learn a lesson so powerful that it will alter the course of our lives and will mold the person we are to become throughout eternity. This is a story about a life altering lesson.

I had known Carolyn since we were toddlers playing together in the park. Every week our moms would sit and visit while we dug in the sandbox. We loved the sandbox. The sandier we got the better we felt. We were princesses of our sandbox castles and I think we fully expected to be real life princesses when we arrived in the adult world.

Carolyn and I maintained our friendship throughout elementary school. We were in a small community with a small school. Everyone in our school was friends with everyone else. There were no real best buddies. Whoever happened to be nearby was your buddy for the day.

As we entered sixth grade our bodies began to change. Carolyn was a little slower to mature than the rest of the girls except for her nose. Carolyn's nose just seemed to grow and grow. I remember taking "bets" with the rest of the kids at school as to just how much Carolyn's nose grew every night.

By the time we were in the seventh grade Carolyn's nose was quite large. None of us ever really looked at Carolyn for who she was as a person. We only saw her as a nose and an opportunity to hone our skills at joke telling. If we would have looked beyond the outside of Carolyn's body, we would have realized there was a loving and caring person on the inside.

Baseball was a major school sport in our community. Carolyn loved the game and she seemed to be a natural. I never knew how or why it all started, but it was decided that Carolyn should be moved into the position of left fielder. It was felt that with her nose there to block the way nothing would get passed her. Carolyn was even dubbed the "Rhino" of Maple Valley.

There was so much talk in our community about our secret weapon "Rhino" that we began to believe as long as Carolyn's nose was in left field we were undefeatable. I think the other schools were even a little intimidated by the mere thought of our secret weapon.

During our eighth grade year Carolyn lost all personal identity. She was simply called "Rhino." Often, Carolyn would have tears in her eyes, but that was easy enough to explain. With that nose she had to have been susceptible to every allergy known to mankind.

At the start of the baseball season, Carolyn asked the coach if she could try playing first base. The coach looked at her and just laughed. He asked if she was kidding. No, "Rhino" needed to stay where she was in left field. We couldn't afford to lose our secret weapon. Carolyn cried for a few days. We all felt she was being very selfish.

As the year progressed Carolyn began to withdraw more and more from everyone. If Carolyn ate lunch she would sit by herself. When we were out of class, Carolyn stood alone underneath the old maple tree. In class, Carolyn sat and stared out the window. The rest of us thought Carolyn was getting pretty "high and mighty." Just because she was the left field secret weapon didn't mean that she was better than anyone else.

Two days before our biggest baseball game of the season, Carolyn was not at school. I remember thinking she had better not be sick and mess up this game. "Rhino" needed to get it together and plant herself out in left field. She could be "high and mighty" if she wanted, but not at the expense of costing us the most important game of the season.

The next day would be one of the saddest days of my life. I would learn a lesson that forever altered who I was and how I saw other people.

As I entered school that day there was an odd feeling in the building. Strange people were everywhere in the hallways. The principal called a special assembly the very first thing in the morning. He took out a piece of paper and began to read a note that was written in very simple handwriting. The note read:

I am sorry I let you down. I just can't go on being a "freak" of nature. I hope I am going somewhere where I will be seen as a person, not just a giant nose known only as "Rhino." When we meet again in eternity please call me Carolyn. That is all I ever wanted to be.

Carolyn Had Committed Suicide

None of us ever saw the sadness in Carolyn, or maybe we choose to ignore it. We treated her as an object—a giant nose. Carolyn felt like a "freak" of nature because we made her feel like a "freak" of nature. Not a single one of us had ever looked past the outside package of Carolyn to the person on the inside. Carolyn had been a very loving caring person who would have done anything to help someone in need.

Grief counselors stayed in our school for several days. In time each of us learned to handle Carolyn's suicide in our own way. Through Carolyn's pain we saw the importance of looking past physical appearance to the person inside the body.

A plague now hangs in the entry of the school. The plague is in loving memory of Carolyn. It reads very simply:

As you look at each of us
see past the outer package
to the gift within

STUDY GUIDE

GLOSSARY OF TERMS

alter—to change

eternity—something that lasts forever

"freak" of nature—a feeling that you are unlike anything else known to mankind

hone—to sharpen

inferior—not as important as something or someone else

intimidated—made to feel inferior

mere—very simple

plague—a wall hanging

repertoire—an accumulation of something

susceptible—easy to come down with something (i.e., a cold; the flu)

undefeatable—not able to lose (i.e., playing a game)

withdraw—to go away from something or someone

PRE/POST DISCUSSION QUESTIONS

The questions are intended to be used before the story to generate a discussion about suicide and after the story to measure any impact the story may have had on the students' views of suicide.

1. Have you ever felt like a "freak" of nature? When?
2. When is it okay to have a nickname for people?
3. How can nicknames hurt a person?
4. What would drive a person to commit suicide?
5. How does suicide affect other people in the community?

Extended Activities:

• Have students practice giving positive accolades about each other.
• Have students rewrite the story allowing Carolyn to play the first base position in the big game.
• Have students write an essay reflecting on how they want to be viewed by others.
• Have students reflect on the special gift that is within themselves.

NOTES

PONDER AND REMEMBER

PROLOGUE

This is a story about the value of a school in the community. The story encompasses a time of happiness and a veil of sadness. This story deals with the great loss that can be felt due to apathy.

Even as a very young child I remember how our community seemed to revolve around the school. School activities were the highlight of the week. If there would have been a reward for the most community members ever to attend school functions, our school would have won above all others.

The school in our community began through the generosity of our pioneering forefathers. They truly believed that the school was the heart of a community and that the community's values were reflected in the school.

Year after year students attended school. One class per grade for twelve grades. Each year there were games and dances to attend. Concert music "rattled" the walls and tumblers tumbled across mats to the enthusiastic roar of the crowd. People held weddings and attended funerals within the grounds of our school. The Fourth of July fireworks could "knock your socks off" and our community Founders' Day Celebration would rival any celebration throughout the state.

No one could have imagined anything on earth that would have brought our school down, but before we knew it we were caught up in a drama that would devastate our community.

My fifth grade year began as any other year had begun. That year though the principal called a special assembly. "Old Bill" needed to talk with us. "Old Bill" was the school custodian. We were sure he had been the school custodian since time began.

"Old Bill" wanted us to know that the school was beginning to deteriorate. There didn't seem to be the respectful atmosphere that had always been there in the past. Students seemed to be displaying an apathy toward the school that "Old Bill" couldn't understand.

We listened attentively to what "Old Bill" had to say and we nodded in agreement. I am sure we all intended to go out and be respectful.

"Old Bill" would see us in the hallway and remind us to be respectful of our school. He just didn't seem to get the idea that keeping the school clean was his job not ours.

What difference did it make if we dropped paper on the floor? "Old Bill" could sweep it up after school. That was his job after all. It was always great fun to throw paper at the trash can to make a "three pointer." "Old Bill" should have appreciated the fact that we were honing our basketball skills by shooting hoops at the trash can.

So what if gum stuck to the floor every once in a while. "Old Bill" had a scraper. It wasn't that tough to scrape up the gum. And why were lines of pencil marks drawn down the hallway such a big deal? At least there weren't swear words on the bathroom walls.

Everyone knew it was much more fun to sit on the desks and tables than to sit on the chairs. Besides being able to put your feet up on the chair while your butt was on the desk was just plain cool. What was the big deal if something broke on occasion? "Old Bill" had pliers and a wrench. School furniture couldn't be that tough to repair.

My fifth grade year ended with "Old Bill" still nagging us about being respectful of our school. We were sure he would calm down over the summer. It had to have been just a bad year for him.

During my sixth grade year we again had a special assembly. That time the principal talked to us. He said that if the respect for our school continued to decline there was a very good chance that the school would close its doors forever.

I remember thinking that I was glad I was not part of the problem. Of course I was always respectful. I didn't write on the walls. Drawing cute little pictures on the bulletin boards wasn't on the walls so that wouldn't be disrespectful. Dropping papers on the floor was an accident. I was busy and didn't mean for the paper to fall on the floor, besides "Old Bill" needed to sweep the floors anyway. I couldn't help it if other people dropped their gum on the floor. It wasn't my gum so why shouldn't I just kick it out of my way?

Two weeks before the end of my sixth grade year the unthinkable happened.

An announcement came out in the newspaper and our superintendent gave an assembly. At the end of the year our school would close its doors forever.

"Old Bill" came one last time to clean the school. He scrubbed and scrubbed until the school was "squeaky" clean. "Old Bill" arranged every desk and chair into perfect rows. He straightened each book on every book shelf in the school.

There wasn't a speck of dust and nothing was left out of order. When he finished, "Old Bill" locked the doors one last time. He was the last person to ever set foot inside what was once a beloved part of our community.

At the start of the next school year we were loaded onto buses to begin the journey to our new schools. We had to ride on the buses for twenty-five miles in each direction. The new schools were big. We were spread out between several schools. We left for school very early in the morning and returned home late.

Our families and community members no longer attended school functions. The school functions were just too far away. People's lives were busy and they didn't have the time to drive the distance. Any students that were involved in school functions were loaded onto buses and bused to the function.

A veil of sadness settled over the community. Occasionally I would see someone standing at the school windows looking in at what was once the delight of our community. Never again did the school doors open. Our school remained exactly as it was when "Old Bill" locked the doors for the last time after his final cleaning.

"Old Bill" himself came to the school once a week for the rest of his life. He would arrive promptly at 7:00 a.m. every Tuesday. "Old Bill" would mow the lawn and pull the weeds. He would sweep sidewalks and wash the outside windows. "Old Bill" never set foot inside the school, but he kept the outside of the school looking well-tended and well loved. At exactly 11:00 a.m. "Old Bill" would sit down under the elm tree and have his lunch. When lunch was over he would stand and look inside the school window. After a few minutes he would turn and walk away. I could only imagine the thoughts that he was thinking.

A stone statue appeared in front of our school one day. No one ever knew where it came from or who placed it on the school grounds. There was a simple inscription on the statue which read:

This School Was Built Through Love and Dedication
It Was Lost Through Apathy

The veil of sadness never really lifted from our community. In time I came to realize that it is the responsibility of each one of us to care for our school. ·Apathy in a school is contagious. A single piece of gum dropped on the floor and kicked out of the way can be the beginning of the end when no one cares.

STUDY GUIDE

GLOSSARY OF TERMS

apathy—showing no concern

atmosphere—a feeling that surrounds you

contagious—a feeling that spreads from one person to another

deteriorate—to begin to fall apart

devastate—to be deeply hurt by something

encompass—to include completely

enthusiastic—to be very excited about something

focal point—the main center

forefathers—the people who first established or started a community

foster—to promote the growth of something

Founders' Day—a celebration honoring the establishment of a community

generosity—to give a lot toward something or someone

honing—sharpening your skills

upkeep—taking care of something to keep it in good repair

veil of sadness—a feeling of great sadness that surrounds something

PRE/POST DISCUSSION QUESTIONS

The questions are intended to be used before the story to generate a discussion about how we show respect for our school and whose responsibility is it to take care of the school, and after the story to measure any impact the story may have had on the students' views of school respect and responsibility.

1. Whose responsibility is it to clean the school?
2. Do students have a responsibility in the upkeep of a school? When?
3. Can a school be the focal point of a community? How?
4. How important is your school in the community?
5. What difference would it make in the community if your school closed?

Extended Activities:

- "Adopt" a bulletin board and foster respect for your school through the displays.
- Spend one class time weekly cleaning up the school.
- Write an essay on the schools importance to the community.
- Write thank you notes to the custodians and maintenance crews.

NOTES

THE ETERNAL SCAR

PROLOGUE

Prejudice. This is a word that can be misunderstood and is often used as an excuse for not getting things the way you want them. In its true form prejudice causes a wound so deep that the pain never heals and the scars are eternal. This is the story of an eternal scarring prejudice.

I had finished my seventh grade year. I was on top of the world. Next year I would be an all-important eighth grader and eighth graders ruled the school. I was one of a few students selected to be in the local big sister/big brother program. The program was designed to help five year olds get ready to enter kindergarten.

My "little sister" was named Rosalia. She had beautiful brown eyes and long black hair that hung down to her waist. Rosalia was very shy and barely spoke at all. She had only been in our town for three months and she did not speak a word of English.

Rosalia and I met each day at school where we joined the rest of the participants in the program. Right from the first day Rosalia and I seemed to become as close as real sisters. As each day ended I could hardly wait for the next day to begin. I was having such a great time with my "little sister."

Each morning Rosalia ran to me with open arms. She'd give me the biggest bear hug and the most beautiful smile in the world. I loved being with Rosalia and I was feeling pretty self-important because surely I was the best "big sister" in the whole program.

About a week after the program started Rosalia spoke her first English words. We were sitting at the lunch table with a group of other program participants. We always ate lunch in a family style setting. I had just passed Rosalia a piece of bread when she looked at me with her beautiful smile and said "thank you"! I was shocked to hear the words, Rosalia was ecstatic to have said them.

After her experience of saying thank you, Rosalia began to say new English words on a regular basis. She talked more and more each day. Rosalia became less and less shy and I knew she would make a great impact when she entered kindergarten.

The big sister/big brother program was going great. Rosalia and I were having an awesome time together. Our awesome time lasted until the Wednesday of our fifth week. That Wednesday would change the rest of our time together and would impact my life in a way I did—not understand until a few years later.

The Wednesday started off just as all the other days had started. Rosalia ran to me in the morning with open arms and gave me a big bear hug squeeze. She told me good morning and said "I love you." I knew we were in for another great day.

The morning passed quickly and it was time to line up to go to lunch. Rosalia and I were in the front of the line. A little boy named Jonathan pushed in front of Rosalia bumping her backward. He turned and looked at her as he stated:

"Little brown jug who is in my way
go back home where you need to stay."

"You look like such a dirty brown
go away and leave our town."

I remember laughing out loud and thinking, "Wow that kid has got some poetry talent." I tugged on Rosalia's arm and pulled her to the back of the line. What difference did it make if we were in the back of the line? There was always plenty of food and it was no big deal.

When I looked at Rosalia's face she was as pale as a ghost. Her smile was gone and for a brief moment I thought her eyes looked "dead." Rosalia didn't say a word. She just stared at the floor. Throughout the rest of the day Rosalia said absolutely nothing.

Rosalia came every day for the rest of the program, but never again did I get a big bear hug from her. She rarely spoke, never smiled and generally kept her eyes staring downward. I left the program on the last day wishing I could see just one more of Rosalia's beautiful smiles.

During the next few years I would occasionally think of Rosalia. It was always a haunting image of Rosalia looking as though the life had been drained from her. I couldn't shake the awful feeling when I thought of her.

Three years passed before I saw Rosalia again. I was sitting in the park when she walked up to me. Rosalia looked at me and simply said, "Why? Why did you laugh when Jonathan called me a dirty brown? You made me go to the back of the line like I wasn't as good as anyone else. I loved you and I thought I was a special person until you showed me that I wasn't even worthy of being in your town." With tears in her eyes Rosalia turned and walked away.

With those words Rosalia had indicated that I was prejudice. I had heard the word prejudice often at school. If you didn't choose someone first to play on your team, you were prejudice. If a teacher called on someone else to answer the question you wanted to answer, he was prejudice. When the cafeteria staff didn't serve your type of food they were prejudice against people with your skin color.

Prejudice was a word that was thrown around as an excuse when things did not go your way.

For the first time in my life I understood what the word prejudice truly meant. Prejudice is judging someone to be unworthy solely because of their skin color, their religion, their language, or some other factor that is different from you. When you are prejudice you do not look inside the person or judge them as an individual. You lump a group of people together and say they are unworthy simply because of a shared single attribute.

Jonathan had been openly prejudice toward Rosalia when he pushed her backward and stated his poem. Without realizing it, I had demonstrated my own prejudice by laughing at Jonathan's poem and by taking Rosalia to the back of the line.

Prejudice is like a knife blade that cuts deep within a person's heart and soul. Eventually the wound closes, but there is always a scar left behind. The scar never heals and it runs as deep as the penetration of the prejudice blade.

I suddenly knew why I had the haunting image of Rosalia. I had allowed a prejudice to show through that targeted her. Rosalia had been a beautiful little girl who happened to have brown skin. By laughing at Jonathan's poem and taking Rosalia to the back of the line I condoned the prejudice message that said it was okay to treat her unworthy simply because she was different from me. Rosalia was cut deep with the knife of prejudice and the scar would be eternal.

STUDY GUIDE

GLOSSARY OF TERMS

attribute—something that is special about a person (i.e., hair color)

barely—not happening very often

condoned—approved of a happening or event

diversity—differences between people (i.e., religion)

ecstatic—very happy

eternal—lasting forever

family style —doing something together as a single group (i.e., eating lunch)

haunting—something that bothers you in an uncomfortable way

indicated—made a choice

participants—people who are a part of something (i.e., game players)

penetration—to go deep inside of something

prejudice—judging someone to be unworthy because of an attribute

unworthy—not important or special

PRE/POST DISCUSSION QUESTIONS

The questions are intended to be used before the story to generate a discussion about the concepts of prejudice and after the story to measure any impact the story may have had on the students' views of being prejudice.

1. What does prejudice mean to you?
2. When is it okay to treat people differently?
3. How do you feel when someone treats you differently?
4. How are people affected when they are treated differently?
5. How could you help someone understand how being prejudice affects other people?

Extended Activities:

- Invite people of different cultures into the class to talk with students.
- Establish pen pals in another country.
- Write essays about foreign countries.
- Display bulletin boards reflecting diversity.

NOTES

A SINGLE SPLIT SECOND

PROLOGUE

Safety concepts. We learn them, we practice them, we use them every day. Each of us though, goes through a time when we feel nothing can happen to us. We are invincible. This is a story about being invincible.

Mom and Dad had always taught me to be safe when crossing the street. From the time I was barely able to walk they took me out and showed me how to cross a street where there was a crosswalk. If no crosswalk was available, we crossed at a spot where we could see the traffic in both directions. We always held hands and I remember feeling very secure with them beside me.

Learning to ride my tricycle was no different. The first time they put all the safety gear on me I thought I would topple over sideways. I rode only in the yard or on the sidewalk in front of our house. Never was I allowed to ride in the street.

On my fifth birthday my parents bought me a shiny new bicycle. The safety gear that came with my bicycle had bright green and yellow flowers. I thought I was the coolest five-year-old in town. I worked and worked every day learning to ride my bicycle and learning bicycle safety.

The first time I was going to ride my bicycle in the street Mom and Dad talked for two hours going over and over bicycle safety rules. I thought my head would explode before we ever got to the street corner. We rode around and around our block making sure I knew and followed all of the safety rules. By the time we were ready to take an actual ride down the street I was too tired and we had to go back home.

When I started school I was well versed in street safety. All through elementary school I practiced the safety rules with my parents, my teachers, and my classmates. I could have taught safety rules on public television.

The day before I entered sixth grade I made an announcement to my parents. I let them know that I no longer needed anyone to hold my hand when I crossed the street. I could ride my bicycle very safely alone and by the way please don't follow me around in the car just to make sure I was okay. In essence I was a big girl now, I was responsible, and I could take care of myself!

I either rode my bicycle or walked to school every day. When I started out I followed every safety rule just as I had been taught. As the year progressed I thought less and less about the safety rules and more about joking around with my friends.

My friends and I always had a great time going to and from school. We would walk down the sidewalk often pushing and shoving each other just for the fun of it. Sometimes one of us would fall off the sidewalk in front of an oncoming car or bus. We were oblivious to the fact that we could have been seriously injured.

When I rode my bicycle to school I always had a feeling of power. Even with my safety gear on I could move down the street like the wind. I got to the point that I darted in and out of traffic with ease. Dashing in front of an oncoming car was a special thrill. Just seeing the terrified look on the driver's face as they narrowly missed me simply fed into my feeling of being all-powerful.

Spring arrived and I could hardly wait for track season to begin. I was a great runner. I knew in my heart that I would someday be participating in the Olympics. Every day I ran or rode my bicycle for two miles just to build up my leg muscles. I was on a roll and I fully expected to take the track team and the world by storm.

The first two weeks of track season had been great and I was awesome. When I ran no one could catch me. I should have run my way into the record books, but instead I rode my way straight into a nightmare.

It was a Saturday afternoon and we had just completed a district track meet. I won my events and I was feeling on top of the world. I had ridden my bicycle to the track meet because I was going to the coach's house for pizza when we were finished. The whole track team would be there and excitement filled the air. We were the champs! Nothing could stop us now.

I left the pizza party feeling totally indestructible. All I could think of was being the star track runner and the fame I was sure to acquire. I saw the car beside me, but it didn't matter. I was fast. Faster than the speed of light I turned and darted right in front of the car. The look of terror on the driver's face simply fed into my indestructibility.

My next conscious memory was of me lying in a hospital bed. My arm was bandaged and my leg was in a cast up to my hip. I opened my eyes to see Mom and Dad standing over me. Tears flooded their eyes and there was a look of sheer panic on their faces.

I think the memory of my next visitor haunted me even more than the memory of my parents. A lady walked into my room. Her eyes were swollen red from crying and she couldn't seem to stop shaking. I learned that the lady's name was Mrs. Green. She had been driving the car that hit me.

Mrs. Green spent the night in the hospital with my parents. She was inconsolable for fear that I would die and she would have been the one to kill me. She cried and cried, begging my parents to forgive her. Between sobs she told them that she just couldn't stop the car in time to keep from hitting me.

Two days later Mrs. Green brought her daughter Hannah to visit me.

Hannah had drawn me a picture and she brought me her favorite teddy bear as a get well gift. Hannah was three years old and she just couldn't understand why her mommy cried and cried. When Hannah handed me the picture she said she hoped I would get better soon so her mommy could stop crying and be happy again.

I stayed in the hospital for three weeks. Hannah and her mom came every day to see me. Hannah would sit on my bed and we would color pictures or play paper dolls. Mrs. Green would sit in the chair. Her eyes were filled with tears the entire time she would be in my hospital room. Mrs. Green spoke very little except to ask for my forgiveness.

After leaving the hospital I spent weeks and weeks in physical therapy. My leg was held together by metal pins and I would always walk with a limp. Dreams of Olympic stardom faded into a recurring nightmare of being hit over and over again by a gigantic bicycle.

I learned that Mrs. Green stopped driving her car and barely left the house. When she and Hannah had visited me in the hospital they walked two miles in each direction to see me. Mrs. Green had once been full of energy as she taught preschoolers how to tumble their way across mats and bounce to new heights on the trampoline. After the accident, Mrs. Green simply spent hours sitting in her chair. Her eyes would fill to the brim with tears as Hannah stood watching and wondering where her mommy had gone.

I was taught every walking and bicycle safety rule known to mankind. Mom and Dad had entrusted me with the responsibility of putting those safety rules into effect. I took their trust and squandered it away, one day at a time, until I finally devastated the lives of two families in a single split second.

STUDY GUIDE

GLOSSARY OF TERMS

conscious—being aware of what is happening around you

devastated—deeply hurt by something

entrusted—when someone puts their trust in you to do the right thing

essence—in reality

haunted—being bothered by something in an uncomfortable way

inconsolable—unable to be comforted due to an event (i.e., a death)

indestructible—unable to be destroyed

invincible—a feeling that you will live forever; not able to be destroyed

minimum—the smallest amount

oblivious—with no thought as to how actions can affect an outcome

physical therapy—treatments to help restore movement after an accident

recurring—happening over and over

secure—safe

sheer—totally

squandered—wasted away

topple—fall over

PRE/POST DISCUSSION QUESTIONS

The questions are intended to be used before the story to generate a discussion about safety and after the story to measure any impact the story may have had on the students' views of safety.

1. Who is responsible for safety on the roadways?
2. Should people be required to have a license to ride a bicycle? Why?
3. Who is affected when there is a bicycle accident?
4. Should bicycles and cars be allowed on the same roadway? Why?
5. Should there be a minimum age to ride a bicycle on the roadway? What age and why?

Extended Activities:

*   Have students design/display a bulletin board on safety.
*   Have students prepare presentations on safety.
*   Have students visit younger students to discuss safety.
*   Have students write an essay about safety.

NOTES

A Shattered World

PROLOGUE

Taunting. It can be subtle or it can be overt. Either way the taunting pushes at a person, breaking down their resistance and altering their perceived world.

This is the story of a perceived world that was shattered by taunting.

I met Nicholas the day we started preschool. He was of a very small stature and the rest of us towered above him. We were drawn to Nicholas from the beginning, the girls most especially. Nicholas was like the dolls we left behind while attending school.

Day after day we tended to the needs of Nicholas. We helped him sit down. We helped him stand up. We carried him from place to place on the playground. If Nicholas was hungry, we gave him our snack. If he was tired, we did his color page. When it was cold, we zipped up his jacket. When it was hot, we helped him out of his sweatshirt. In essence we did it all.

Year after year we propagated a dependence on us by Nicholas as we created a person in our desired image. We never left him alone or gave him the opportunity to make discoveries of his own. We openly issued invitations to Nicholas for any event that was happening in our lives. We planned his birthday parties for him and gave strong opinions on his every movement. In reality we ran his life.

Nicholas was enthralled with all of the attention. Even though we ran his life, he felt the world was revolving around him. It was unimaginable that anything could ever shatter "the world of Nicholas."

We entered fifth grade teaming with excitement. We were in a new school with new expectations and new classmates. During our fifth grade year we grew, we matured, and we developed new friendship guidelines.

By the time we entered sixth grade, we had evolved into new people.

Nicholas on the other hand appeared to have remained virtually the same. He was still of small stature and still waited for the world to revolve around him. Nicholas wanted our full attention and we became unwilling to give it.

As the year progressed, we began to join together to taunt Nicholas. We were tired of his demanding ways. He needed to realize that the world did not revolve around him and that there were times we did not want him to tag along with us.

It was easy to taunt Nicholas due to his desire to be our friend and to be the center of our world. The taunting continued to intensify every day. By the end of the school year Nicholas was relegated to spending his day in the "protective custody" of the bathroom.

The relentless taunting continued into the summer. A group of us had gathered at a local swimming hole where the rocks were high and the water was deep. By chance Nicholas was there waiting to join our fun.

Most of us never fully realized that Nicholas could not swim. We just joined in the taunt to push him toward the edge of the rocks and into the water below. In an instant Nicholas would descend into a world of darkness and I would descend into a world of unrelenting remorse.

It took three years, four months, and six days for Nicholas to awaken from his coma. Beyond all odds he awoke and made a near full recovery. His speech was left slurred and his right arm was in a continuous state of weakness. Nicholas left our school and left our community. His family took him to a place where he could build a new world.

I spent three years, four months, and six days trying to comprehend why. Why I would have been a part of taunting someone. Taunting them beyond endurance. Taunting the person who had been my friend. The person whose life I helped run and whose character I helped create.

Nicholas had been born premature, nearly died, and in the end marveled the doctors with his determination to survive. He never let go, never stopped trying, and never wanted anything but acceptance.

By not standing up for my friend and by participating in the taunting, I allowed the near destruction of a person who only wanted to be a part of my life. With my thoughtless actions I squandered away a friendship and aided in the shattering of a world.

STUDY GUIDE

GLOSSARY OF TERMS

aided—helped

altering—changing

alternative—a different choice

coma—not aware of your surroundings; in a state of sleep

comprehend—to understand

continuous—always happening

dependence—relying on someone or something

descend—to go down

determination—making sure something will happen

endurance—able to keep something happening

enthralled—very happy about a situation

essence—in reality

evolved—changed into

guidelines—rules for use

marveled—was amazed

overt—happening with full knowledge

perceived—the way you thought something was happening

premature—born earlier than expected

propagated—helped to grow or develop

"protective custody"—in a place where it is safe

relegated—being put into a certain place or position

relentless—not stopping

resistance—trying to avoid a happening

shatter—to break apart

slurred—not speaking clearly

squandered—wasted away

stature—size

subtle—hardly noticeable

taunt—to put pressure on someone to break down their resistance

unimaginable—unable to believe that something could happen

unrelenting remorse—continuous sadness; feeling continually bad about a situation

virtually—totally

PRE/POST DISCUSSION QUESTIONS

The questions are intended to be used before the story to generate a discussion about the effects of taunting and after the story to measure any impact the story may have had on the students' views of taunting.

1. What does taunting mean to you?
2. Can taunting ever be a good thing? When or why?
3. Does taunting ever really hurt anyone? When or how?
4. Can you taunt someone and still be their friend? How?
5. Can you push someone beyond endurance by simple taunting? How?

Extended Activities:

• Have the students rewrite the story beginning in the fifth grade.
• Have the students do presentations on the effects of taunting in a school setting.
• Have the students design a bulletin board using acceptance as an alternative to taunting.
• Have the students write an essay about the effects of taunting.

NOTES

From Indifference
to Acceptance

PROLOGUE

Bullying. We have all witnessed it and for some of us we have experienced it. By a demonstration of indifference to bullying, we display an acceptance of the bullying. This is the story of an indifference that led to an acceptance that led to a tragedy.

Joey entered kindergarten overweight. I remember thinking "this kid must be a second grader just visiting our class." I would watch with the other students as Joey struggled in and out of his jacket or to climb the stairs of the playground. I always worried that Joey would fall, roll down the stairs, and lay there like a turtle on his back missing the entire recess. I had visions of the teacher using a small crane to lift him upright again.

Right from the beginning students would taunt Joey about his weight. There were always comments about how much he ate, how he would break a chair if he sat on it, or how he needed two spaces when sitting on the carpet.

By the time we entered middle school the taunting turned to bullying. Joey was quite large by now. Something called "a glandular condition" was said to be the culprit for his weight problem. Joey was craving friendship, but most students either ignored him or bullied him.

The bullying slowly evolved from stealing Joey's hat on a routine basis to greeting him every morning as he entered school. The bullies took what they wanted from Joey's lunch and actually reached into his pockets to take any money that he had in his possession.

By virtue of being timid and passive, Joey would never acknowledge to anyone what was happening to him. If adults showed concern, Joey always stated that everything was fine. He had a lot of buddies and couldn't be happier. In reality, Joey would sit alone in his room shedding tears nightly before lying down to escape into a world of slumber.

Unknown to the rest of us, there was a turbulence building within Joey. The turbulence would fester and one day erupt into an electrifying explosion that terrified a school and shattered a community.

As we entered high school the bullying made another evolution. The Internet was looming and there was a sophistication in using it. One day, about midway through the school year, the bullies took pictures of Joey in the school locker room showers and then posted them on the Internet. Pictures went into the niche of the cyber world depicting Joey in a state of nudity and as a "loser."

Joey became aware of the pictures on the following day as he entered a classroom and approached the students at the back of the class. He stared at the computer screen and never uttered a sound. Instead his fists clenched and his body began to tremble.

Joey was not at school the next day and no one questioned why.

Friday morning arrived and the day started on an even keel with any other school day. Students gathered in the courtyard preparing for the day and for a jump start to the weekend. Joey arrived in the courtyard and made his way to a group of students. He stood silently staring and then in a flash, terror rang out through the school.

As two students lay dying, Joey turned the gun on himself. When the frenzy cleared, a note was found pinned to his shirt. Written in a plain elementary script Joey simply stated, "All I ever wanted was acceptance. Acceptance to be a friend. Acceptance to be me."

In time I came to realize my part in the bullying of Joey. Never once in all the years I had known Joey did I stand up for him. Even though I was aware of the bullying, never once did I report it to an adult. Never did I say hello to Joey or even ask if he needed help. Because of my indifference, I sent out a subtle message that promoted acceptance of the bullying.

In my school there was an indifference that led to an acceptance that led to a tragedy.

STUDY GUIDE

GLOSSARY OF TERMS

bullying—treating someone with total disrespect to put pressure on them

clenched—held tightly together

craving—a strong desire for something

culprit—the person or thing that is responsible for an event

depicting—representing something

electrifying explosion—a disturbance that is very upsetting

elementary script—printed text

even keel—when two things are the same

evolved—changed into

evolution—making a change

fester—to become more upset about an event

frenzy—in a confused state of being

glandular condition—a problem with the glands in the body

indifference—not caring about something

justified—approved to happen

looming—something that is ready to happen

niche—a specific place where something happens or where something lives

passive—not fighting or showing aggression

routine—happening on a regular basis

slumber—in a state of sleep

sophistication—wise; able to direct someone or something else

subtle—hardly noticeable

taunt—to put pressure on someone to break down their resistance

timid—very shy

tremble—to shake

turbulence—a disturbance or violence beginning to happen

uttered—made a sound

virtue—because of something else

visions—happening in a person's mind

PRE/POST DISCUSSION QUESTIONS

The questions are intended to be used before the story to generate a discussion about bullying and after the story to measure any impact the story may have had on the students' views of bullying.

1. How does bullying affect someone?
2. Is there ever a time for bullying? When?
3. Why do people bully others?
4. Does bullying someone else make you important? Why or why not?
5. Can you bully someone and be their friend at the same time? How?

Extended Activities:

- Have the students rewrite the ending of the story.
- Have the students write an essay about bullying.
- Have the students practice giving positive accolades about each other on a daily basis.
- Have the students design a bulletin board showing acceptance vs. bullying.

NOTES

DOMAIN OF TERROR

PROLOGUE

Internet predators. They have a sophistication that allows them to gain confidence and to establish a domain in which to groom the innocent. This is the story of an Internet predator and his Domain of Terror.

I was thrilled when my parents announced that it was time for me to have my own computer and that the computer should be housed in my bedroom. Yes, a computer would enhance my homework capabilities, but having my own computer would mean a new found freedom in my junior high existence.

Although I was the last of my friends to get a computer, I thought I was well versed in computer usage. I had spent countless hours at my best friend and neighbor Jenny's house. We would sit in her room with the music cranked up as loud as allowable and let our fingers soar over the keyboard as we played games and browsed the Internet for the latest teen clothes available.

When my computer arrived there were appropriate guidelines set for my use of the computer and definitely there were limits as to what Internet sites I could access. I assured my parents I knew the rules and understood their concerns.

My house became the focal point for Jenny and me to use the computer. My parents both worked and were not home until dinner time which left Jenny and me about three hours of "freedom time." The rule was homework first and then we could have our "freedom time." "Freedom time" for us meant computer time.

At first Jenny and I were very cautious. We were careful not to put any information into the computer that might identify us and we stayed away from any personal sites. As time went on, and after many discussions with our friends, Jenny and I decided to set up our own personal space accounts. After all, what could happen? Only invited guests would view our sites or interact with us. Unknown to us was our level of naivety.

Our naive understanding of the computer world launched us into invigorating discoveries and into the depths of a cavern from which we could not fully ascend.

The personal sites we set up were complete with pictures. We loved posting pictures of ourselves just having fun. There were pictures of us in swim suits, in our "jammies," in T-shirts and jeans. We had pictures from all over town. Pictures of us in front of our school, at the city pool, beside the movie theater, and one of us pointing at the "Welcome to Our Town" sign.

Along with our personal sites, Jenny and I loved to enter the teen chat rooms. Our chat room friendships grew larger day by day. We were ecstatic on the day our new friend Cedric entered the chat room. Cedric was sophisticated. There was no other way to describe him. He was on the verge of getting his driver's license and would be a junior in high school the next year.

After two weeks of chatting with Cedric, Jenny and I invited him into our personal spaces. This meant we shared pictures with him and he shared pictures with us. Cedric was awesome! We had never known anyone like him before.

Jenny and I shared everything, but she did not share the one single detail that would impact and change her life forever. Jenny agreed to meet Cedric in person. She would meet him in a remote park at the edge of town. Cedric felt it was better this way since I might be a little jealous when realizing he liked her the best. Jenny was only protecting my feelings as she went to meet Cedric alone.

My family and I were out of town on that fateful day. As we arrived home, about 10:00 p.m., we observed flashing lights illuminating our neighborhood. The lights were coming from Jenny's driveway.

Jenny was last seen by her family at 9:00 a.m. on that Saturday morning. She was not seen again for two days. Her crumpled, near lifeless body was found in a ravine four miles from the remote park at the edge of town. Jenny had been beaten, sexually assaulted, and left for dead. She was simply thrown out like a bag of trash.

The first day I was allowed to see Jenny in the hospital my blood ran cold. One leg and both arms were in casts. Her lips were swollen and she had very few teeth left in her mouth. Jenny was unable to sit up and she stared straight ahead through black swollen eyes. Jenny did not utter a single sound.

In time Jenny's outer body healed, but her inner spirit had been shattered. The once vibrant Jenny now spends her days sitting in a rocking chair behind locked doors as she reminisces about the days gone by. Too terrified to leave the house, Jenny became an agoraphobic.

Jenny and I had been groomed by a professional predator whose domain was the computer Internet. Cedric was an older man who gained accessibility into our lives by posing as a teenager with sophistication. He knew precisely what to say to us and how to separate the two of us.

It was not difficult for Cedric to pinpoint a location for Jenny. The pictures we innocently posted on our personal spaces gave him all the clues he needed. Cedric had the names of our school, the city pool, the movie theater, and most importantly the name of our town.

Cedric remains elusive and continues to prey for naive innocent young girls on the Internet while Jenny remains in a Domain of Terror.

STUDY GUIDE

GLOSSARY OF TERMS

accessibility—able to be reached or contacted

agoraphobic—a fear of being in open spaces (usually remains in the house)

appropriate—something that is okay for the situation

ascend—to rise up

"blood ran cold"—a saying meaning something was terribly bad

browsed—looked something over

capabilities—what you are able to do

cautious—very careful

cavern—a deep hole

depths—deep down inside of something

domain—specific area that you are living or working in

ecstatic—very happy

elusive—not able to be found

enhance—to make something better

fateful—an event that occurs without having any control of the event

focal point—the main place or idea

groomed—prepared someone to easily follow your directions

guidelines—rules for use

illuminating—very bright with lights

invigorating—very exciting

launched—set in motion

naivety—not comprehending or understanding something

posing—pretending to be someone else

predator—someone who goes after another person to hurt them

prey—the person targeted to be hurt

ravine—at the bottom of a canyon

remote—far from anything else

shattered—broken apart

soar—to fly over

sophisticated—wise; able to direct someone or something else

utter—to make a noise or sound

versed—having a complete understanding

vibrant—full of life; excited about life

PRE / POST DISCUSSION QUESTIONS

The questions are intended to be used before the story to generate a discussion about predators and after the story to measure any impact the story may have had on the students' views of Internet predators.

1. What does predator mean to you?
2. How does a predator gain access to a victim?
3. Is it easy to be a predator over the Internet? How?
4. How can you protect yourself from a predator?
5. Is it safe to post pictures on the Internet? Why or why not?

Extended Activities:

- Have the students do research and a presentation on Internet predators.
- Have the students write an essay on Internet predators.
- Have the students rewrite the ending of the story starting with Jenny's choice to go to the park.
- Invite a guest speaker to talk to the students about Internet predators.

NOTES

Brink of Disaster

PROLOGUE

Choices. We all make them. Some choices we make follow the guidance of a mentor. Some choices we make are small and have little or no repercussions. Some choices we make are significant and can lead us to the brink of disaster. This is a story about a disastrous choice.

Molly and I met the first day of second grade. We were both new to the school and had arrived before any other students. I think it is safe to say that I doubted we would ever become friends. I was timid and just stared at her. Molly on the other hand looked as though she wanted to send daggers my direction. Every morning we went through this same ritual. I stared and she sent the daggers.

We were in the same class and spent five months making certain we did not utter a word to each other. Finally the inevitable happened. Molly and I spoke to each other! It was a cold snowy morning in February and the teacher decided the two of us should share the job of taking a small box of books to the library. With each of us carrying our side of the box, we were determined not to look at each other or to speak. We made it to the library door without a single sound.

It is hard to imagine, but that simple trip down the hallway changed our lives forever. As Molly and I stood at the library door not communicating, we tried to figure out how to open the door while holding the box. In our struggle, the box crashed to the floor and books went everywhere. We both ended up sitting on the floor and just couldn't help but laugh at ourselves and at each other. Our trip back through the hallway found us laughing so loudly that the fourth grade teacher stepped out of her class to give us a very stern look.

The hallway trip launched Molly and I into an incredible friendship that took us to the brink of disaster and returned us to the reality of a life's decision.

By the time Molly and I landed as freshmen in high school, we were inseparable. She was an avid soccer player and I was her avid fan. In reality, I think Molly was destined for soccer stardom. During the off season when Molly wasn't playing soccer we loved to chat on the phone, gossip, and watch movies. We especially loved movies that could bring a tear to our eyes. We would bet each other about who would shed the first teardrop. The loser of the bet bought the next bag of chips.

Somewhere along the way we began to enjoy drinking wine. Our first wine tasting started as a whim. We were visiting my aunt for the weekend and everyone else in the house was asleep. We were watching an especially emotional movie and decided a small sip of wine from the open wine bottle on the counter would enhance our viewing pleasure. We enjoyed the taste of the wine and this opened the door to an increasing desire to have more.

Anywhere we went we scouted for wine that we could access. It wasn't hard to access the wine and we increased our consumption to match the wine availability. By the time we were juniors in high school we could have been considered to be "winos." The need for wine was consuming our thoughts.

Summer came and we were ecstatic at the thought of being seniors. We were prepared to complete our senior year and then take the world by storm. Unfortunately, one fateful summer evening turned the storm into a tumultuous hurricane that would obliterate our dreams forever.

Molly and I were to attend a summer beach party. It was to be the "bash of the year." Much to my chagrin, I got sick the day before the party. I was too sick to get out of bed so Molly sadly went on without me, promising to give me all of the details.

For Molly the party meant a large consumption of wine. She drank her way through the party and then took a wine-filled water bottle for the long lonely car trip home.

Molly and I had driven the same lonely stretch of road a million times, but on this fateful night she "failed to negotiate" the curve. Molly flew in her car for one hundred fifty feet before landing in the ravine. She lay "broken" in her car for three hours before help arrived.

It took two days before I was well enough to visit Molly in the hospital. It was unbelievable. The shock I felt upon entering her room was astounding. My best friend's body was shattered and she would never walk or even feed herself again. Molly was now a quadriplegic.

Day after day Molly and I spent hours blaming everyone else for her accident. The road designers should never have made that sharp of a curve. Why hadn't the county officials put up a sign demanding a lower speed zone. Wine makers shouldn't allow people to drink any wine. We could come up with every excuse to blame someone else.

In reality we were the ones responsible for our decisions. Molly and I made our own choices. We had made the choice the first time to drink and Molly made the choice to drink and drive. We alone took ourselves to the brink of disaster.

STUDY GUIDE

GLOSSARY OF TERMS

astounding—very surprising

avid—wanting to do something all of the time

brink of disaster—on the edge of being destroyed

chagrin—very upset about something

consuming—eating or drinking something

consumption—having eaten or having drunk something

communicating—talking with each other

daggers—small knives

destined—bound to happen

disastrous—causing much suffering or loss

ecstatic—very happy

enhance—make something better

"failed to negotiate"—was not able to drive around the curve

fateful—an unhappy event that occurs without having any control
of the event

incredible—very wonderful

inevitable—will happen no matter what

inseparable—not wanting to be apart

launched—set in motion

mentor—someone who teaches you

obliterate—destroy

quadriplegic—someone who is paralyzed from the neck down

ravine—at the bottom of a canyon

repercussions—events that happen based on previous events

ritual—happening on a regular basis

shattered—broken apart

significant—very important

sole—only

timid—very shy

tumultuous—disorderly; all churned up (i.e., tumultuous storm)

utter—total (i.e., utter silence)

whim—without previous thought

"world by storm"—thought of as being an important person or event

PRE/POST DISCUSSION QUESTIONS

The questions are intended to be used before the story to generate a discussion about drinking and after the story to measure any impact the story may have had on the students' views of drinking.

1. Does it really hurt someone to sneak a drink of wine or alcohol once in a while if they are underage? Why?
2. Winc is made from grapes. Should wine be considered as an alcohol? Why?
3. Should wine or alcohol be kept in a locked cabinet? Why?
4. Whose responsibility is it to stop someone from drinking?
5. When do you have sole responsibility for the choices you make?

Extended Activities:

- Have students write an essay about the effects of drinking.
- Have students do a presentation about drinking and driving.
- Have students rewrite the story with a different ending.
- Invite a guest speaker to talk with students about drinking and driving.

NOTES

TORN ASUNDER

PROLOGUE

Drugs. This is a word familiar to each of us. Some drugs are legal and help us when we are ill. We call these prescription drugs. Some drugs are illegal and can alter our mental status. We call these street drugs. This is the story of a brother, a street drug, and a family torn asunder.

My brother Michael was four years old when I was born. From the time I could walk I thought the sun rose and set in him. He was my mentor and the core of my universe.

Michael taught me how to ride a bike, Rollerblade, skateboard, and to throw the fastest softball in the county. He grew up following the rules and making sure I followed them as well. We crossed the street at the corner, said please and thank you, did our homework, and always obeyed Mom and Dad. I don't ever remember Michael being in trouble and consequently, with his guidance, neither was I.

By the time Michael was a freshman in high school, he was a star athlete with stellar academics. Opportunities abounded for Michael. Everyone wanted to associate with him and I, by virtue of being his sister, was a shining star. It was unfathomable that anything could ever change our universe.

The change was subtle at first. Hardly noticeable. Michael was irritable at times, but who wouldn't be with a whole universe revolving around you. His athletic abilities began to falter ever so slightly, but that was explainable by sheer fatigue. Michael's grades began to slip and some of his conversations didn't make sense. Easy enough to explain. When you are on top of the world people just don't comprehend your thoughts.

Michael finished high school and headed to college. As the year progressed we began to hear less and less from him. He never answered his phone and decided to stay away during the holidays. Mom, Dad, and I were distraught without Michael's presence in our home.

Unknown to us, Michael left college in the middle of the year and moved into a house with seven other people. We received phone call after phone call from old friends trying to locate him. Michael appeared to have dropped into oblivion.

Six months went by with no word from Michael. Mom, Dad, and I kept ourselves functioning by adhering to the old adage that "no news is good news." Michael must be doing okay. He was just too busy to call home. We would hear from him soon.

The phone rang once, and then it rang twice. Unexplainable shivers ran down my spine. Never in my life could I have imagined that one single phone call would be the beginning of the end in a life I had once known with my beloved brother Michael.

Before I knew it we were in the car racing toward Community Hospital. We drove one hundred miles at a speed that could have broken the world record. Mom couldn't stop crying and Dad clenched his teeth. I was numb, unable to fathom what was happening.

A doctor greeted us at the hospital emergency room entry. He let us know that my brother would be unrecognizable and that in essence his welfare was currently in the hands of the state mental health department.

Unknown to us, my brother Michael had been doing illegal drugs. He had done enough drugs that his mental capacity was now diminished. The damage was done and there was no going back to the Michael we once knew. He stayed in the hospital for three weeks before being released to exist on his own. It was determined that Michael was not a danger to society.

As time passed, Michael's mental health vacillated between being in a "vegetative" state and being in a state of confusion. He was unable to continue his education or maintain a job.

Michael's home has become a place on the street of our small community. He remains in a general state of disorganization where he is unwashed, unshaven, and residing with his fellow street patrons.

Occasionally Michael comes by our yard to say hello. He never comes inside and never stays long before the confusion sets in. Michael spends his days gathering enough cans to subsist on a meager diet before he lies down on the cold hard earth to sleep.

Once I had a brother who was my mentor, my life, my universe. Love tied us together, but drugs tore us asunder.

STUDY GUIDE

GLOSSARY OF TERMS

abounded—was full of

adage—an old saying that has been around a long time

adhering—to stick to something

associate—to be close to someone (i.e., be close to your friend)

asunder—apart or widely separated

clenched—held tightly together

comprehend—to understand

confusion—not understanding

consequently—something happens because of something else happening

core—the middle of something

diminished—got smaller and smaller

distraught—very upset

essence—in reality

exist—to be

falter—began to get worse

fathom—to understand

fatigue—to be very tired or worn out

guidance—to show the way

harmful—something that will hurt you

irritable—easily upset by things around you

meager—a very small amount

mental capacity—your ability to comprehend things or events

mentor—someone who teaches you (i.e., how to play ball)

oblivion—a place that is unknown

sheer—totally

stellar academics—very high grades; very smart

subsist—to survive on

subtle—hardly noticeable

unfathomable—completely unable to understand

unrecognizable—not able to know who the person is

vacillated—went back and forth

"vegetative state"—not comprehending anything around you

welfare—well-being

PRE/POST DISCUSSION QUESTIONS

The questions are intended to be used before the story to generate a discussion about illegal drugs and after the story to measure any impact the story may have had on the students' views of illegal drugs.

1. Can illegal drugs have a harmful effect on someone? How?
2. Can you always tell when someone is on illegal drugs? How?
3. Can illegal drugs ever be helpful to someone? When or how?
4. Do people who do illegal drugs deserve to live on the streets? Why?
5. Is there a way to help someone on illegal drugs? How?

Extended Activities:

- Have students research and do a presentation on illegal drugs.
- Have students write an essay on illegal drug use.
- Have students rewrite the ending of the story.
- Have a guest speaker talk with the students about illegal drugs.

NOTES

ABOUT THE AUTHOR

Cleresse A. Sprague is a parent, a grandparent, and an educator with twenty-five years of classroom teaching experience. She holds a master's degree in special education with a focus on behavior intervention. Mrs. Sprague's teaching experiences include working with students and their families in the realm of headstart, migrant headstart, elementary school, middle school, and junior high school. She has taught both general education and special education classes.

The *Intertwining Choices Social Stories Curriculum* evolved from daily interactions Mrs. Sprague had with students and their families. The social stories, which are timeless and yet require diversity, were written to address issues that students struggle with on a daily basis during their formative years.

Cleresse A. Sprague has a passion for providing a diverse avenue that could enable our youth and their educators to traverse from the world of social confusion into a world of clarity and empowerment.